Pursuing God

A Seeker's Guide

PURSUING GOD

A Seeker's Guide

Jim Elliff

Christian Communicators Worldwide

ISBN 0-9745253-0-8

Scripture taken from The Holy Bible, New King James Version.

For information regarding additional copies of *Pursuing God*
and other publications, write:

Christian Communicators Worldwide
201 Main Suite #3
Parkville (Kansas City) MO 64152
USA

Email: info@CCWonline.org
www.CCWonline.org

Cover design by Thomas Jones

Jim answers questions for seekers at
www.WayToGod.org

A small group discussion guide
for *Pursuing God* can be found online
at www.CCWonline.org

Contents

Pursuing God

Twenty-one Days with God
A Bible-reading guide

Introduction

I lost him!

For a few agonizing moments, my son was nowhere to be found. I ran up and down the aisles of the store yelling out his name. All I could think was, "abduction!"

Nothing would stop me from finding him—nothing!

Few, perhaps, have sought God frantically like I sought my boy. Yet what is to be found is even more important, as hard as that might be to imagine. It is an eternal relationship with God Himself, forgiveness of sins, life in heaven, meaning out of chaos. God told the Old Testament people, "And you will seek Me and find Me, when you search for Me with all your heart" (Jeremiah 29:13).

Some of you may experience *moments* of intensity about becoming a true Christian, between periods of relative peace. But the desperate need is there always, underlying all that you do and say.

Others pursue God like a child playing "hide-and-seek." To them it is intellectually stimulating to think about God, but it is not for real. True seekers, however, are not playing a mental game.

This book is for you, the seeker. You fully *intend* to know Him. It is not a book attempting to convince you that God is there, or that Christ is who He says He is. Another book will have to deal with those matters.

Rather, this book is for the person who knows God is there, and believes that somehow he must relate to Him. But how?

Though these chapters are brief, they are meant to carefully guide you into a better understanding of the problem of sin, the dangers, the solution, and the assurance of life in Christ.

In a way, each chapter stands alone, but together they present something much fuller. I will attempt to make the profound as simple and understandable as possible. But still, it is God himself, ultimately, who must open your eyes. So pray as you seek.

At the end of this book is a plan to help you read the book of John. This will give you the actual words of Christ to help you know Him. You may want to ask a friend or mentor to meet with you weekly to discuss your questions.

Once the early Christian leader Phillip spoke with an Ethiopian man in the desert. Although the man was reading the Bible, he did not understand its message about Christ. "How can I unless someone guide me?" he said.

This book is my way of guiding you to Christ.

Jim Elliff
Kansas City, Missouri, USA

What does God think of me?

The answer to this question might surprise you—and disappoint you. But the disappointment is necessary. If you do not fully understand the awful predicament that sin puts you in, you may never appreciate Christ's coming, death and resurrection enough to become a Christian. Think of it this way. You cannot be healed through the help of a doctor unless the doctor first diagnoses the problem. You have to hear the bad news first. But the benefits of this understanding are inestimable and eternal.

The first two chapters are about the kind of person you are without Christ. In the third chapter you will read about God's anger toward those who will not come to Him on His terms. Nobody was ever converted to Christ without knowing, and feeling deeply, the terribleness of sin and his or her desperate need for Christ.

As you read, ask God to help you understand the problem of sin and God's just disposition toward it.

Chapter One

So What's the Problem?

A well-known Christian philosopher, Francis
Schaeffer, was asked this question: If you had
only one hour on a train to tell someone about Christ,
what would you do? He answered: I would spend forty-
five minutes showing him the problem, and fifteen
minutes showing him the solution.

Do you have a problem? Perhaps it is not so easy for
you to see. If you have good relationships, have an en-
joyable profession or make good grades, have a family
that loves you, and feel hope about the future, then you
may not think there is anything to be fixed. But there is.
Your problem is with God, and it is serious enough to
cost you everything good for all of eternity.

You may not feel your problem right now. A man may
be condemned as guilty and yet not feel guilty, just as a
person might have cancer and not feel it or even know
it. There is real or legal guilt and there is emotional
guilt. But regardless of how your emotions are experi-
encing your dilemma, God makes it clear that you have
an insurmountable problem.

So what's the problem?

The Bible uses several words and phrases to help us
understand. First, it says you are DEAD—not sick, not

desperately sick, not sick to the point of death, but *dead*! The consequence of sin in each person is spiritual death, according to the Bible. "The soul who sins shall die" (Ezekiel 18:4). "For the wages of sin is death . . ." (Romans 6:23). In fact, the Bible teaches that we are born as sinners (Psalm 51:5; Romans 5:19).

God means that every person starts out spiritually as a walking dead man. He may be alive on the outside, but inside he is dead to God. Only Christ can make him alive. So the old story that says salvation is like a Christian throwing a lifeline out to a drowning man is not the truth. It is worse than you thought. You're not drowning, you're face down on the ocean floor!

Second, the Bible says you are BLIND. "But even if our gospel is veiled, it is veiled to those who are perishing, whose minds the god of this age has blinded . . ." (2 Corinthians 4:3-4). Just as a person in a cave cannot see his hand in front of him when there is no light, so you cannot see Christ without God shining his light on Him (see vs. 6). In a world of sightless people, everyone imagines his own inward reality, but he cannot see the truth unless God gives him sight.

The Bible says that you are LOST. In Luke fifteen Jesus described lostness by telling the stories of the lost sheep, the lost coin, and the lost son. There is nothing more hopeless than being lost. Like the man in a blinding snow storm, every turn seems right for the moment, but all is futile.

The Bible also says that you are CONDEMNED. This means that you are under the judgment of God for your disobedience against Him. ". . . But he who does not believe is condemned already . . ." (John 3:18). God condemns every unbelieving person to hell, even if he or she is in the remotest part of the world. He is just in doing so, because unbelievers have sinned against whatever knowledge of God they have (see Romans 1).

What I am trying to say is that you do have a problem, and it is the type of problem that can only be solved with help from the outside. As a dead person you cannot make yourself alive; as a blind person you cannot give yourself sight; as a lost person you cannot find your way out; and as a condemned person, you cannot absolve yourself from your actual guilt. You have a problem and you really don't have a solution unless it comes from someone else besides you.

Trying to overcome your problem on your own is a useless exercise. The famous preacher of the 1700s, George Whitefield, once said, "What! Get to heaven on your own strength? Why, you might as well try to climb to the moon on a rope of sand!" You simply cannot accomplish what God requires.

How does God solve your problem? First, He sets His heart on you from eternity past. Think about that! What an exciting thing to know that God has forever loved people just like you. "I have loved you with an everlasting love" (Jeremiah 31:3).

Next, He sends His Son, Jesus Christ, to cover the cost of your sins by dying on the cross in your place. "But God demonstrates His own love toward us, in that while we were still sinners Christ died for us" (Romans 5:8). In Christ's death the full payment for all the sins of all who come to Him are fully met. In this way God's justice is satisfied and you are pardoned. This is why Christ is called the Savior, or the Rescuer.

Finally, He pursues you by His Spirit, convicting you of your sinfulness, teaching you about the nature of salvation, and drawing you to Christ's beauty and worthiness (see John 16:9-11; John 6:44, 45). Christ becomes irresistible to you. The Bible teaches that even the faith you exercise is a gift from Him (see Ephesians 2:8-9).

You have a problem and God has the solution—the only solution.

The people who have experienced this solution are called believers. They believe that God has loved them from eternity past. They believe that the payment of Christ on the cross for sins was for them. They find Christ irresistible, and following Him the greatest privilege of all. They have faith in Christ and what He has done for them. They trust Christ, looking outside of themselves to Him alone. They believe.

"Therefore, to you who believe, He is precious."
(1 Peter 2:7)

Chapter Two

You Don't Look So Good

When humorist Erma Bombeck saw her new passport photo, she gasped, "Anyone who looks like *that* is too sick to travel!" Getting a good look at yourself can be deflating to say the least.

It might surprise you to know that when you look in the mirror in your bathroom you don't really see yourself. You see the exact *opposite* of yourself. Your left ear is on the right side and your right ear is on the left side. Spiritually, most people think that they are looking pretty good, compared to others. But are we seeing the truth?

Physicist David Thomas made a curved mirror in 1975 that actually reflects the correct image of the one staring at it. The Bible is that kind of mirror for the soul. When you look at it, you will see exactly what you are like before God.

What does the Bible say you look like?

Paul gathered some Old Testament Scriptures to make an accurate portrait for us. He said,

> There is none righteous, no, not one;
> There is none who understands;
> There is none who seeks after God.
> They have all turned aside;
> They have together become unprofitable;
> There is none who does good, no, not one.
> (Romans 3:10-12)

You're not righteous. Jesus once called some of the most religious people of His day, "white-washed tombs filled with dead men's bones"—not very flattering, but perfectly accurate from the Holy One's perspective. One man may *appear* to be righteous before another man, but before God there is no one truly righteous. The only righteousness that God accepts is His own. To stand before God in our own righteousness is certain rejection.

You have no understanding. A professor may give a lecture on "The Nature of Biblical Conversion" and state every fact accurately, yet not understand. When he comes into the teacher's room he may ridicule the beliefs he just articulated, and call them foolish. Should we really believe he understands when he rejects Christ as God, and the death of Christ as essential to salvation? He knows his facts about salvation like one knows trivia. But if he *understood* it, he would see himself as the fool and Christ as his only hope (see 1 Corinthians 2:14).

You have no desire for God. It is one thing to seek happiness and meaning in life; it is quite another thing to seek God. Jesus said that people do not naturally come to Christ. "And this is the condemnation," He said, "that the light has come into the world, and men loved darkness rather than light, because their deeds were evil" (John 3:19-20). If you are a seeker, really desiring to solve this eternal problem, you can be sure that your desire for God initiates with God Himself (see John 6:44).

You are rebellious. "All have turned aside," the apostle Paul said. The blame for being outside of God's family belongs to you. You have a nature that turns away from Him and seeks to live independently. Paul said, " . . . the carnal mind is enmity against God; for it is not subject to the law of God, nor indeed can be" (Romans 8:7).

You have become unprofitable. Like meat left on the table overnight, the Bible states that man without Christ is really worthless. This does not mean, of course, that God does not have a purpose for you. After all, he even used Judas (see Acts 4:27-28). But it does mean that you will live and die meaning nothing for the Kingdom of God. It is obvious that God is not impressed with one's status in the world.

Paul goes on to give more of God's view of you in picture words almost too stark to accept at first. Note, as you read, the emphasis on *destructiveness* and *deceitfulness* as the true nature of the non-believer. These two characteristics are easy to find in our culture.

> Their throat is an open tomb;
> With their tongues they have practiced deceit;
> The poison of asps is under their lips;
> Whose mouth is full of cursing and bitterness.
> Their feet are swift to shed blood;
> Destruction and misery are in their ways;
> And the way of peace they have not known.
> There is no fear of God before their eyes.
> (Romans 3:13-18)

Are you and your friends really like this? Before you answer, remember that the Bible often describes the individual from the heart (1 John 3:15). The hidden things are the real things to God. For instance, people who love violence and bloodshed in the movies are at *heart* bloodthirsty. And the person who hates is a murderer before God, which Christ made clear in no uncertain terms (Matthew 5:21-22). He also said that lust is adultery in the heart (Matthew 5:27-28).

And, remember, given enough pressure all that is in the heart will come out. Jesus states, "You are of your father the devil, and the desires of your father you want to do. He was a murderer from the beginning, and does not stand in the truth, because there is no truth in him. When he speaks a lie, he speaks from his own resources, for he is a liar and the father of it" (John 8:44).

The real problem with man is that he cannot get out of this awful mess alone. He cannot overcome his sinful nature. Paul asserted, ". . . all are under sin." Being a refined sinner or even a religious one is still being a sinner.

But the good news comes in right at this point. Christ died for sinners like you and me! Though you are deserving of God's wrath, Christ completely satisfied the just wrath of God toward sin for those who will put their trust in Him. That won't mean too much to you as long as you think that you are looking pretty good. But when you see yourself as you really are, you will find Christ's death for sinful people the greatest news you have ever heard.

Chapter Three

Is God Angry Anymore?

When I was in public high school, we had to read part of a famous sermon called *Sinners in the Hands of an Angry God*, by the early American pastor, Jonathan Edwards. He graphically pictured sinners as spiders dangling by a thread over the fire of hell. He also asserted that God is angrier at this moment with some who are living than with others who are already in hell.

Do you believe that? Is God angry? I don't believe my teacher thought so. When I later studied the Bible on the subject, however, I was surprised by what I found.

I learned that God's anger is pure. The biblical command, "Be angry and do not sin" reminds us that there is an anger that is justified. God always has this kind of perfect, holy anger.

The apostle Paul said, "For the wrath of God is revealed from heaven against all ungodliness and unrighteousness of men . . . " (Romans 1:18a).

King David said, "God is a just judge, and God is angry with the wicked every day" (Psalm 7:11).

And the apostle John said, "He who believes in the Son has everlasting life; and he who does not believe the Son shall not see life, but the wrath of God abides on him" (John 3:36).

Note that these verses teach that God is not only angry with sin but also with the sinner. Since God sees everything, He evaluates perfectly (Hebrews 4:13). Whenever God is angry it is for holy reasons.

Sometimes we think of God as a judge sitting on the bench who passively issues punishment to guilty persons. But is God like this? The original words used for God's anger are passionate words. Why? Because, unlike our judges, God Himself has been sinned against.

Notice the emotion in Nahum 1, where God is identified as jealous, avenging and filled with wrath (verse 2). Verse 6 is even more pointed. "Who can stand before His indignation? And who can endure the fierceness of His anger? His fury is poured out like fire . . . "

However, even in the midst of His fury, God is self-controlled. The Bible teaches that He is slow to anger (Nahum 1:3), and most of us learned long ago that God is love. But while a loving God certainly is willing to hold off His judgment, it is just as certain that He will judge sin.

Romans 2:5-6 describes it this way: "But in accordance with your hardness and your impenitent heart you are treasuring up for yourself wrath in the day of wrath and revelation of the righteous judgment of God, who 'will render to each one according to his deeds.'" In verse 16 of the same chapter it says that this will occur "in the day when God will judge the secrets of men by Jesus Christ . . . "

Why is God so angry? There are at least three reasons.

1. Because of the sheer number of your sins. If you were to sin only 10 times a day for one year, you would disobey

God 3,650 times. But if you sinned 10 times a day for 15 years, you would sin 54,750 times! You are a professional sinner! Yet, how many times did Adam sin before he was cursed by God?

2. Because you have sinned against the greatest being and the highest command. There are different levels of sin and punishment (Luke 10:12; 12:42-48). A crime is weighed according to the seriousness of the command and the stature of the person who is sinned against. It is one thing to disobey your employer at work or your coach at school. It is another thing to disobey a judge. It is one thing to turn in a late term paper. It is another thing to murder the president. The highest command is to "love the Lord your God with all your heart, mind, soul and strength" (Mark 12:30). The greatest being is God. Each time you sin, you commit the highest crime against the greatest being! God ought to be angry.

3. Because you have sinned against God's greatest act of love. Christ was sent into the world of men and women out of love (John 3:16). But many of your friends, and perhaps you also, have rejected Christ up to this very moment. This rebellion is a sin against compassion. Is it any wonder that God is angry with those who think little of His love?

How can you be rescued from this holy anger? Only through propitiation. But what does that mean?

The word "propitiation" (pro-pish-ee-ay-shun; sometimes translated, *atonement*) means this: Jesus fully satisfied the just anger of God for people like you by dying in your place, taking on Himself all the wrath you deserve. We learn about this in Romans 3:24-25 and Hebrews 2:17. God's just fury, indignation, and anger for sins were poured out on Christ for every sinful person who will come to him by faith.

And that is great news!

How long do I have to make up my mind?

The fact of sin and judgment just presented, as terrifying as it is, often does not stir those without Christ. Why? Because they believe they are secure and will not die. Seekers are also often unaware of the nearness of Christ's coming. If you lack passion about coming to Christ, perhaps these next three chapters on the brevity of life may guide you to Him. I want you to see that you must come to Christ now. Nobody has ever benefited from waiting, and nobody is guaranteed a future opportunity.

Chapter Four

If I Should Die Before I Wake

Did you pray these words as a child?

Now I lay me down to sleep.
I pray the Lord my soul to keep.
If I should die before I wake,
I pray the Lord my soul to take.

There is a candor in this little prayer that makes you shudder. It seems strange to hear little children pray these words when they have only begun to live.

This prayer recognizes two ultimate realities: We will die, and there is something good beyond death that the Lord may take us to. But it implies another truth—the Lord will not take everyone there.

If a man or woman is sane and thinking, the fact of death aggravates the mind. Its certainty stirs up at least a chronic uneasiness, and in times of vulnerability or danger may do even more. It is a frightening fact when one chooses to face it honestly. The Bible calls death an enemy. Most people fear it, and they are right to do so.

There are those who can say that death is not a worry. True Christians, that is, those who have come to Christ on His terms and are genuinely converted, have a certain right to say this, as we will see. But others are only bluffing themselves. They either believe themselves to be invincible or they think that merely *saying* they are not afraid alters the facts. Both thoughts are deceptions.

We have a ticking heart—an internal battery with no electrical cord leading to an outlet. And the One who has the power to keep it going has no compelling reason to sustain our heart one minute longer. Rather, most people are steadily increasing the number of their sins against the only One who can keep them alive and take them to heaven. That's scary.

But it doesn't have to be that way! Christ came to liberate you from such fear.

Christ appeared, said the writer of Hebrews, to "release those who through fear of death were all their lifetime subject to bondage" (Hebrews 2:15).

Christ takes the binding fear out of death by turning it into an advance rather than an eternal loss. He makes death the ticket to life.

Here's how that works. Along with everybody on the face of the earth, you are constantly sinful. These thousands of sinful thoughts, words, and actions cause the perfectly holy God to judge you as deserving of hell. But Christ's death in the place of sinful people, as a true substitute, provides the way of escape. God pardons the one who comes to Him because Jesus took the punishment in his place. In simple terms we may say that the just penalty for sins either falls on you or Christ.

The person who comes to Christ rejects the life he was living to become Christ's own child. He comes by faith. That is, he rests all his confidences for eternity on

Christ alone as the only One who fully satisfied God's justice on the sinner's behalf. This is called *believing in Christ*. And the one who believes has no need to fear death anymore. The judgment for sin has been covered by the Substitute.

Jesus said, "He who believes in Him is not condemned; but he who does not believe is condemned already, because he has not believed in the name of the only begotten Son of God" (John. 3:18).

The Christian knows physical death will come. He can look it straight in the face. To be certain, he will not enjoy the pain of the dying process, but death itself is not the problem. As a Christian he knows that he will be in heaven after he dies. Like the apostle Paul, he asserts, "to die is gain" (Philippians 1:21).

A Jewish oncologist in one of our Southern states saw this phenomenon. In fact, he converted to Christianity because of seeing the difference in how Christians and non-Christians die.

Perhaps it would be helpful for you to meditate on the following words that Christ gave us about life and death. He said these words to Martha, the sister of Lazarus who had just died. And as you carefully think over this profound set of words, remember that Christ is the only legitimate antidote to the fear of death because He is the only one who can say, "I am the life." Here are His words. Believe them—believe in *Him*.

> I am the resurrection and the life. He who believes in Me, though he may die, he shall live. And whoever lives and believes in Me shall never die . . .
> (John 11:25-26)

Chapter Five

Sooner Than You Think

A few years ago a Chicago news station reported a local skydiving incident. The video showed the skydivers jumping out and maneuvering into position from the vantage point of the open door of the plane.

While still filming, the cameraman made his jump. Within seconds the camera was jerking wildly up and down and side to side as it plummeted to the ground. Reaching for his ripcord, the terrified diver discovered that in his excitement he had forgotten to put on his parachute! The black, silent end of that video clip was the tragic reminder of the suddenness of death.

The day of your death will arrive right in the middle of your plans. Those skydivers planned to have a great experience, to celebrate, and to go home to sleep. But God had other plans for them. He may have other plans for you as well.

God warns the overly confident planner through the author James: "Come now, you who say, 'Today or tomorrow we will go to such and such a city, spend a year there, buy and sell, and make a profit;' whereas you do not know what will happen tomorrow. For what is your life? It is even a vapor that appears for a little time and then vanishes away." (James 4:13-15)

James states two absolutes that must be considered whenever you make plans. The first is this: You do not even know what will happen tomorrow.

A friend of mine got up one morning to ride his all-terrain vehicle prior to breakfast. Most likely his coffee was still brewing when the ambulance came to take his dead body away. He had plans, but he did not know the future.

The second inescapable fact, James notes, is that "Your life is just a vapor"—that warm moist release of air out of your mouth on a cold day. It is there, and then it is not. Whether your life is a shorter "hhh" or a longer "hhhhhh," it is still only a nanosecond in terms of eternity.

At our family reunion I noticed my boys playing around the exposed roots of century-old trees in front of the farmhouse. I thought to myself, "I used to play on those same roots."

I also remembered how my aunts and uncles seemed so ancient to me when I was a boy. But then I calculated, "I'm the very age they were! And most of them are dead!" Life moves by *very* quickly.

The above facts create an understandable fear for any person who will seriously contemplate them. But wait a minute! There is another fact that James brings to the table. And this fact completely overwhelms the first two. Simply put, it is this: Whatever happens is entirely up to God!

It is true that we are prone to say, "Today or tomorrow we will go to such and such a city, spend a year there, buy and sell, and make a profit." But God says that we *ought* to say something very different.

"Instead," James says, "you ought to say, 'If the Lord wills, we shall live and do this or that'" (James 4:15). In other words, it is up to God whether we live or die, and it is up to God whether we do this or do that.

If we fail to say (and, of course, *believe*) the phrase, "If the Lord wills," then all of our planning is just boasting and bragging about something over which we have no control. Worse yet, such planning without recognizing the sovereignty of God is sin (see James 4:15-16). I don't believe that we have to wear out the phrase every time we speak about the future, but the sentiment must certainly be there. And what you believe you do speak.

In the famous novel, *Kidnapped*, the young hero is being chased by brigands in a crumbling old castle. He makes his way up the stairs in the blackness, one step at a time. Yet we can see what the hero cannot—the next step he plans to take is not there!

Is your next step there? And if you die, are you ready for what follows?

The Scripture says, "Man is destined to die once, and after that to face judgment . . . " (Hebrews 9:27). Plan as you will, you will avoid neither.

In the light of the certainty of death and the uncertainty of life, doesn't it make sense to put your trust in Christ who is called "The Rock of My Salvation?"

In 2001, when race car driver, Dale Earnhardt, made his last turn around the Daytona 500, did he know he would be in an accident that would take his life? Will you? Where will you be when you die? Will you be in a hospital room? On a sports field? Pinned in a car? Will a sign come out of heaven stating, "This is the moment of your death?"

One thing is sure—that time will come, and sooner than you think.

A relationship with God through faith or trust in Christ (which the Bible calls "believing in Christ") is the answer to the insecurity of our earthly life. You must be able to live, even if you die. And you must have a life after death that will never end. Christ provides both.

Remember that Jesus said, "He who believes in Me, though he may die, he shall live. And whoever lives and believes in Me shall never die . . ." (John 11:25-26).

Chapter Six

A Thief in the Night

A friend of mine slept through a robbery in his own home.

His wife wasn't so out of it. In fact, when the man entered their bedroom, she immediately began chasing him down the hall. With this lady on his tail he didn't steal much but trouble. Meanwhile, back in bed, my friend snored away, totally oblivious to the whole ordeal.

The day of the Lord will also come like a thief in the night. Are you ready?

> But concerning the times and the seasons, brethren, you have no need that I should write to you. For you yourselves know perfectly that the day of the Lord so comes as a thief in the night. For when they say, "Peace and safety!" then sudden destruction comes upon them, as labor pains upon a pregnant woman. And they shall not escape.
> (1 Thessalonians 5:1-3)

Notice the word—*sudden!*

He will come while people are saying, "Peace and safety." In other words, life will be going on as normal, with no particular reason to be alarmed. But then, *all of a sudden*, destruction will come.

My mother's childhood home had just been painted. All the older members of the family had worked so hard on it. Now, they would just do a little clean up and then they would be able to enjoy the fresh look. But, *suddenly*, when a fire was started in the fireplace to burn some debris, the room burst into flames. In a matter of a few moments everything was destroyed.

When God's day of judgment comes, most people will rise from bed as on any other day, go to work or school, eat their meals, speak to their friends, etc., just as they have always done. A regular day is precisely the kind of day God will come in judgment. Don't expect someone to announce, "Everyone will now need to prepare for the Day of Judgment. You have 48 hours to get right with God." We don't know the date or the times when destruction will come—we only know that it is destined to happen, and *suddenly*.

The other day I saw a news report of a woman who gave birth to her baby in the car on the way to the hospital. All of a sudden the birth pangs came. Here was this frantic dad trying to get to the doctor in the speed of light while simultaneously telling his wife to hold it in. "Holding it in" didn't work. When the birth pangs come, the baby follows. God's day of judgment will come suddenly, just like that. Now read further—

> But you, brethren, are not in darkness, so that this Day should overtake you as a thief. You are all sons of light and sons of the day. We are not of the night nor of darkness. Therefore let us not sleep, as others do, but let us watch and be sober.
> (1 Thessalonians 5:4-6)

The day of the Lord will *come* as a thief, that is, suddenly. But it shouldn't surprise *the Christian* like a thief. That is, the day of the Lord should not catch any true believer unaware or off-guard as if he were unprepared. A Christian, that is, a true believer, is not like those who sleep, but like those who are "sons of the day." Believers, therefore, should be "alert and self-controlled," fully anticipating such a day of God's wrath and indignation on the world.

For one thing, God has not appointed authentic believers to receive that wrath. "For God did not appoint us to wrath, but to obtain salvation through our Lord Jesus Christ," the writer goes on to say (1 Thessalonians 5:9).

God's children may go through all kinds of physical pain even to the point of death, but it will not be punitive for the believer. For believers, death is the turnstile into God's presence. Some of those believers may even be transported out of it all, without even the smell of smoke. Destruction or death for the non-believer, on the other hand, will always lead to eternal hell, whenever it comes.

Are you one who thinks you can quickly work things out with God as soon as you see trouble is brewing? Then the main point of this passage is directed toward you. The Day will come so suddenly that you will not be able to do anything to alter your destiny. If you go into this time as an unbeliever, don't expect the slightest opportunity to remedy that situation once judgment comes.

But there is hope!

The author, Paul, says that Christ, "died for us, that whether we wake or sleep [here he means, "whether we are alive or dead"], we should live together with Him" (1 Thessalonians 5:10).

Christ's death on the cross is the one means by which you may escape the penalty for sins you deserve. When Christ went to the cross, He did so in order to bear sins and take on Himself God's wrath as a substitute for people like you. Because of that loving, sacrificial act, you may escape the just penalty of your sins and live forever with Him—the deliverance promised to anyone who puts his or her trust in the Rescuer.

And then *sudden* is no longer a frightening word.

Can God change me?

The Bible author Paul called the news about Christ's ability to deliver us from sin and death, "the power of God." That's what you need—God's power. Only a power that strong can change your life. After explaining that reality in a general sense, I've taken sexual sin as a case in point to encourage you to come to Christ even if your sin is enormous.

Pray that you will see and believe in the power of God, no matter what your sin has been.

Chapter Seven

Gospel Equals Power

In the mountain town of Buena Vista, Colorado, my brother and I saw something we had only dreamed could happen. Only three weeks earlier we had been invited to come to the town by a handful of teen-age kids, not much younger than we were, who had just come out of the drug culture to Christ.

These students envisioned filling up the gymnasium in the high school with anybody they could persuade to hear us tell them about Christ. It was completely unorganized. Their advertisement was their changed lives. We were shocked to find the gym packed with people. In the middle of the floor was the painted logo for the school—*The Demons*.

By the time the days and nights of speaking were finished, perhaps two hundred had professed faith in Christ. Students chanting "One Way" down the school hallways would raise their hands with their index finger pointing upwards. Every gathering was charged with a joy and seriousness that was contagious. In this unforgettable experience, we saw something of the transforming power of the gospel.

Whether the message comes to one or to many, it is potent. If you have seen those who have been radically changed by this message, you know what I mean. It can happen to you! Read what Paul says about it:

For I am not ashamed of the gospel of Christ, for it is the power of God to salvation for everyone who believes, for the Jew first and also for the Greek. (Romans 1:16)

In the 1950's, post-war children eagerly listened to the popular radio series called Superman. He was "faster than a speeding bullet, could leap tall buildings with a single bound," and could "stop a powerful locomotive," but even this Superman could not do what God can do—deliver a person out of the kingdom of darkness into the kingdom of light.

There are limits to what *we* can do. A friend of mine, now a professor in a seminary, used to lift weights in a gym with some of the Dallas Cowboys football team. When attempting to dead lift 1000 pounds, he completely herniated and has not been the same since. Yet God has no limits. We simply cannot forgive a man's sins, or make his dead soul alive—but God can.

What makes the gospel so powerful? It is the reality that Christ lived the perfect life we could not live, that He died on the cross as God's perfect Son to bear the sins of sinning and damned people just like us, and that He rose again to conquer the dominance of sin and death. That reality is powerful because there is nothing else to substitute for it—nothing else that does the job that Christ did before His holy and just Father.

Paul himself is an illustration of this power. He was on his way persecuting Christians when God turned him fully around—all of a sudden he loved the very Christ he had been seeking to persecute. How do you explain such a transformation unless you attribute it to the power of God?

When I was a grade school kid, toy makers sold cheap rockets that were powered by air pressure. Perhaps you have seen the plastic rockets that sit on a platform to which you attach your bicycle pump. The harder you pump, the higher it goes.

Becoming a Christian is not just pumping a little religion into your life so that you feel a "lift" when you are emotionally low. Salvation is about coming out of death to life, about being transformed as a person into something entirely new, about being forgiven for the sins that have damned you, about having eternal life. You need the power of God for that.

In fact, you need a power that will take you all the way to heaven! The gospel, according to Paul, is just that— it is the power of God Himself for the complete salvation of everyone who turns by faith to Him.

Never limit God!

Chapter Eight

Destroying the Future

The opposite sex—like any high school or university student, I had dreams of finding just the right one of that variety to spend my life with. In my dreams the standards were reasonable enough—brains, wit, stunning beauty, winning personality, the blindness to think I was great, and an exciting walk with God.

But for many of my friends, the dreams turned to nightmares. Sex prior to marriage took them on a helicopter ride that eventually smashed them on the hard pavement, seriously diminishing their chances of having a marriage that was pure and exciting—not to mention, lasting.

What happens after sex? Do earlier actions decimate a good future?

Sadly, in many cases, the answer is "yes." Our actions do have consequences. Explosives that are loaded into life today may be detonated at the most inopportune times. Like dreaded land mines, they often leave little behind of what promised to be so good and right. Sex prior to marriage, for instance, has a long history of breeding distrust in marriages and causing divorce.

It goes without saying that experience often leads to habit. A person having sex outside of marriage is easy prey for more. Although we are shocked when we hear that someone had an adulterous affair, it is probable that he or she had a sexual habit, mental or physical, for some time prior. A secretive lifestyle of disobedience often comes from the initial taste of the stolen waters of sex—one experience or thought producing another and another, dulling the conscience and weakening the resolve.

The biggest problem with promiscuity is that it ends up in eternal ruin. Paul says in 1 Corinthians 6:9-10 that the wicked will not inherit the kingdom of God:

Do you not know that the unrighteous will not inherit the kingdom of God? Do not be deceived. Neither fornicators, nor idolaters, nor adulterers, nor homosexuals, nor sodomites, nor thieves, nor covetous, nor drunkards, nor revilers, nor extortioners will inherit the kingdom of God.

You may fool others, but you cannot fool God—so don't deceive yourself. Sin leads to judgment. It is true that every person has sinned and deserves hell, but here Paul is making a case for steering clear of the top ten temptations facing the Corinthians, a culture apparently much like our own.

But God can change a life of sexual promiscuity. After cataloging some types of people who will not enter heaven, Paul continues:

And such were some of you. But you were washed, but you were sanctified, but you were justified in the name of the Lord Jesus and by the Spirit of our God. (1 Corinthians 6:11)

There is a lot of hope here. Once caught in the web of lust, does a perpetually sinful lifestyle have to be your only option? No, through Christ you can be liberated—and that's not too strong a word. Though there can never be perfection in the Christian this side of heaven, there is a huge reversal. A true Christian will be able to say, "Because of Christ, that's what I was but not what I am!"

God washes, sanctifies and justifies—just what you need to escape the dictatorial rule of your sinful desires and to be assured of heaven.

When God washes you, He forgives your sins, removing the guilt. That is, through Christ's death He wipes away the guilt and gives you a clean heart. Guilt is not only emotional, but is also *real*. It's good for the feeling of guilt to be removed, but the true problem is the *actual* guilt.

He sanctifies you. That is, God "sets you apart" to Himself as exclusively His. And after setting you apart for His own use, He can make you like Him through the Holy Spirit He puts inside you. This is like God stamping His name on your forehead to designate that you are His child forever.

And God justifies all who come to Him. Justification means that, even though you are a sinful person, you are nonetheless declared righteous in God's eyes, not because of what you have done or not done, but on the basis of what Christ alone has done. His death for you is accepted in place of your death. You are justified by faith in Christ's work and not your works.

It would be wrong of me to say that sexual activity outside of marriage will not cause you serious trouble. As tantalizing as it seems for the moment, failure to follow God's prescription for sex is a formula for calamity. But coming to Christ by faith changes things. When God washes, sanctifies, and justifies, you are not the same anymore. And you're guaranteed a future in heaven as well.

When a friend of mine came out of the hospital after surgery, you could see the improvement in his physical stamina. He was like a new man. But there were scars. Those scars remind him what his body used to be like.

Sexual scars may remain to remind you, but your former failures cannot destroy you if you come to Christ. Like a caterpillar that sheds its cocoon, you can leave that behind forever.

When a person is sick, the doctor may prescribe medicine. What heals the man? Is it the medicine, or his reaching out for the medicine? Christ is the only solution for your problem of sin and judgment. He is the medicine. Who else but Christ can rescue you and bring you into the forgiven family of God? He is the exclusive way to God. He is a narrow way, but a sufficient one.

But how do you reach out to Christ? By repentance and faith. The chapters following explain each of these significant words. And this is exactly what you must do— repent and believe in Christ, on the basis of what He did for people just like you. Even though the Bible describes repentance and faith as graces given by God for which you can thank Him, it is your responsibility to act. You will know that you have these gifts by your actual repenting and believing.

Up to this point you have not repented, nor have you believed. The choice to wait has been yours. And if you wait until a later date once more, and then do so again and again, it will soon be obvious that you never intend to come to Christ. The Lord says, "Seek the Lord while He may be found, call upon Him while He is near" (Isaiah 55:6). There are those who seek a little while, but who never find, because their seeking is only surface, and their love for themselves is permanent.

Chapter Nine

The Change of Mind

The young man was dying—without Christ.

"I have a habit," he said, as he looked up from the bed that had been moved into the living room for his last few weeks on earth. "I know that it is sin and that God does not permit it. I want to continue my habit, however, and I honestly don't intend to stop it. On the other hand, I desperately want to go to heaven. May I become a Christian?"

How would you answer this question?

I responded by saying that it was impossible for him to be converted to Christ while at the same time loving his sin. It is true that anybody who comes to Christ will come with sin. In fact, he or she will come precisely because of that sin—that is, to be rid of it and its awful result. But to come to Christ while loving and cherishing sin is totally impossible. It is like an airplane trying to fly in two directions!

Was I being cruel? No, in fact I was as loving as I possibly could be. I wanted the man to know the truth about repentance because Jesus had said, "I tell you . . . unless you repent, you will all likewise perish" (Luke 13:3).

When the apostle Paul walked up Mars Hill in Athens to contend with the philosophers of his day, he was perfectly frank about their need to repent. He courageously declared that God "commands all people everywhere to repent" (Acts 17:30 NIV). If God demands repentance from *all people everywhere* then you and I are also included.

What is repentance?

To repent means to "change the mind." But this change of mind is not *merely* a new way of thinking about Christ and salvation. It is much more profound, affecting the deepest attitudes and actions.

When a person repents, he comes to God hating what he once loved and loving what he once thought so little of. Such an intense change in thinking about sin and Christ results in believers doing "works befitting repentance" (Acts 26:20). As a person thinks, so he or she acts.

Once a man came to Jesus who was obviously impressed with Him. He got on his knees to ask Jesus an important question. "What shall I do that I may inherit eternal life?" (Mark 10:17)

Jesus' answer was just the reverse of what you would imagine. He said, "You know the commandments: 'Do not commit adultery', 'Do not murder,' 'Do not steal,' 'Do not bear false witness,' Do not defraud,' 'Honor your father and mother.'"

> And he answered and said to Him, "Teacher, all these things I have kept from my youth."

Then Jesus, looking at him, loved him, and said to him, "One thing you lack: Go your way, sell whatever you have and give to the poor, and you will have treasure in heaven; and come, take up the cross, and follow Me."

But he was sad at this word, and went away sorrowful, for he had great possessions.
(Mark 10:20-22)

Do you think Christ was also cruel in what he required? Not so. In fact, the passage specifically tells us that Christ loved him. But this man had another god—Money. Jesus knew that no man may come to Him while simultaneously worshipping another god. "You cannot serve God and Mammon (Money)" (Matthew 6:24).

The man wanted eternal life, but not enough to give up his favorite god. Rather, he rejected Christ for his money, even though he was sad he could not have both.

Christ showed the man that even though he perceived of himself as a person who kept God's laws, he really was a law-breaker. After all, he broke the first command—"You shall have no other gods before Me" (Exodus 20:3).

This story is an illustration of a man who needed to repent, just like the first man described in this chapter. Unfortunately, both of these men, to my knowledge, refused to give up their cheap god for Christ. Both, therefore, went to hell.

Do you remember what Jesus said? "Unless you repent, you will all likewise perish" (Luke 13:3). He requires repentance from you just as he did from these two who died.

You must reject your gods whatever they are—money, sex, sports, sinful habits, hobbies, relationships, even your own self—anything that contends with Christ's rightful place in your life. What may be good and beautiful under the authority of God, becomes a damning idol if you love it more than Christ.

Will you repent and come to Christ by faith? Or, will you stubbornly hold on to a god who will drag you to hell forever?

Christ is not cruel in His offer. He gives you abundant life, forgiveness of all your sins, the Holy Spirit to live in you, a family of loving believers, understanding of the greatest book ever written, and eternal life in heaven—all for the repenter.

Even a dog recognizes the difference between the rancid old chicken bone in his mouth and the fresh T-bone steak set before him.

Repent now and come to Christ.

Chapter Ten

Trying or Trusting?

I was astounded. I had just explained to a group of nuclear scientists the difference between trying to earn salvation by our own works and trusting Christ for it. I thought that I had made myself exceptionally clear. As I left, however, one man thanked me and remarked, "I guess I just need to try harder to be a Christian." He had missed it completely! Why couldn't he see my point?

He had as much hope of getting to God by his human effort as by a space shuttle. Without the aid of the Holy Spirit and the understanding provided only through the Bible, every man reasons that he must *earn* God's favor. The Bible does not say that. It teaches that salvation is a gift, "not of works, lest anyone should boast" (Ephesians 2:9).

The ancient patriarch Abraham discovered that being accepted as righteous before God, (called justification), does not happen by our good works, but through the exact opposite—faith alone. This faith is not in what we do for Him, but in what Christ has done for us.

"For if Abraham was justified by works," says Paul, "he has something to boast about, but not before God. For what does the Scripture say? 'Abraham believed God, and it was accounted to him for righteousness" (Romans 4:2-3).

If you could be accepted by God on the basis of your works there would be reason to boast. It would mean that you never sin. Since, however, we have never known anybody who is perfect outside of Christ, the "works" way to heaven must be the *impossible* way. But there is a *possible* way to be justified—through belief or faith, just like Abraham.

Once, after finishing a meal with some friends, I asked, "Where's the bill? I'd like to pay for your meals." "You can't pay for them," my friend said. "No, please," I insisted, thinking that he was just being polite. "You can't pay," he clarified, "because the bill has already been paid!"

Should I have tried to pay for the meals anyway? Even if I could have forced the cashier to take some money, it would not have changed the bill. It was paid by another, and nothing would alter that. Instead, I took him at his word and rested in what had been done for me.

Christ has fully paid the debt of those who are His. When He suffered and died at Calvary, everything was done for man's sin that could be done. This was an act of the greatest possible grace. For you to think that you could be accepted by your own efforts at being good makes light of the cross of Christ. Paul said, "I do not set aside the grace of God, for if righteousness comes through the law, then Christ died in vain!" (Galatians 2:21).

If you will ever be justified or accepted as righteous before God, then you will have to come God's way, through faith in Christ and what He has done for you. "Trying to be a Christian" is an insult to God and is a way of despising what Christ has done on the cross.

Friends of mine watched a catastrophic event from a hill just above the Guadalupe River in Texas. A bus full of high school students had just come off the hill in order to cross the bridge below. Because of rains upstream the bridge was covered with water, but, with the high wheel wells of the bus, the driver thought he could make it easily enough. Just as they were halfway across, however, a wall of water slammed into the side of the bus and toppled it over into the pounding river.

Soon the students were attempting to maneuver out of the submerged bus. Some made it; others did not. Those who got out were swiftly carried downstream, attempting to hang on to the rocks wherever they could get a hold. They would not last long.

Helicopters from a San Antonio military base were on the scene within moments. A line from the helicopter was fastened around the students making it possible for them to be lifted up and over to dry land some distance away.

One girl was nearly insane with fear. When the soldier got to her, it was only with the greatest difficulty that he was able to get the harness around her. As she was being lifted up into the air, high above the ground, her arms were flailing wildly—so wildly, in fact, that she slipped loose from the harness. My friends watched as she plunged to her death below.

Had she only trusted, she could have been saved.

God will never reward the self-effort you exert to save yourself. He will not let you make the cross a meaningless act. He will not obligate Himself to save you because you do what you believe are good works. But there is a *possible* way because of Christ—the way of faith.

> "Now to him who works, the wages are not counted as grace but as debt. But to him who does not work but believes on Him who justifies the ungodly, his faith is accounted for righteousness." (Romans 4:4-5)

What has happened as you have been reading this book? Do you find that God is calling you to Himself? Are you eager to follow Christ?

This final chapter may help you understand what is happening. Spending some important days in the Bible book of John using "Twenty-One Days with God" (page 59) will help you even more. No one should reject Christ without reading His words. The next pages may be some of the most important for you.

Chapter Eleven

What Shall I Do?

If you have read to this point, you have shown a serious interest in the most crucial issue you will ever face. What should you do now?

In one sense that question is not worded correctly. A seeker becomes a true Christian because *God* does something, creating desire for Him and distaste for sin. If God is at work, you cannot help rejecting your independence and coming to Him. You will place your trust in Him because there is nothing else left to trust. You will love Him because He is irresistible to you.

You will reject your life of disobedience and autonomy because you cannot bring yourself to love such a life any more. Interest in that kind of life has died and you cannot make it live again. You cannot love what you now despise. You can only love what has become lovely.

Once a large group of people who were following Jesus in order to see his miracles and to hear his wisdom turned and left Him in disgust because of something He had said. They could not appreciate or receive what He was saying. These disciples (meaning only "followers" but not true Christians in this passage) could not believe the truth about Christ. Here is what happened:

> And He said, "Therefore I have said to you that no one can come to me unless it has been

granted to him by My Father." From that time many of His disciples went back and walked with Him no more. Then Jesus said to the twelve [original apostles], 'Do you also want to go away?'

But Simon Peter answered Him, "Lord, to whom shall we go? You have the words of eternal life. Also, we have come to believe and know that You are the Christ, the Son of the living God." (John 6:65-69)

The Holy Spirit had arrested the minds of these men (excluding Judas, which Jesus goes on to explain) and they could not help but believe and follow Christ. This fact is significant for you.

You may be saying the same thing. When the question is put to you, now that you have read and thought this through, do you have to say, "I do, in fact, trust Christ, and I do, with joy, reject a life independent of Him"? Can you say, "I place no hope in anything else other than Christ for my salvation"? And are you willing and quite happy for this benevolent God to be the master of your life without rebellion? Do you desire to follow Him, whether difficult or easy, throughout your entire life?

These are the affirmations of an authentic child of God.

If this is true for you, you should tell someone else who is spiritually wise. A Christian friend, pastor, or mentor should know of your change in thinking. Ask them to help you as you begin your new life with Christ.

As you start your life in Christ, you will see the results of this work of God in your attitudes and behavior. You will not be perfect until heaven, but you will view sin and the Lordship of Christ in a very different manner than you used to. When you do sin, ask God to keep you pure and to give you strength to resist temptation. He is able and willing to help.

You will want to find a church that will appreciate what has happened and can guide you. And you will want to be faithful in that church, asking questions, and learning as much as possible. As you might imagine, not every church is the same. At a minimum, attempt to find a church that takes seriously what God says about salvation through faith (not works) and teaches the Bible faithfully.

It is most important to read the Bible and pray. A guide to the book of John and the rest of the New Testament is found in this book. It is helpful if you can meet with a Christian leader or friend who can hear your questions and talk with you about this great book of the Bible. You will be thankful for all you learn.

As you read your Bible, you will find that new converts to Christ were baptized in water as a first act of joyful obedience to Christ. Jesus said that you should be baptized as an outward symbolic declaration of new life in Christ. The church you attend can guide you through the Scriptures on this important and exciting way of expressing your faith.

Talk to your friends and family about what you have found in Christ. You will have a love for them that perhaps you have never known before. God might use you to help them understand what it means to be an authentic Christian.

Jesus gave this commission to his followers. You will find in these words the plan you should seek to carry out the rest of your life.

> All authority has been given to Me in heaven and on earth. Go therefore and make disciples [new believers] of all the nations, baptizing them in the name of the Father and of the Son and of the Holy Spirit, teaching them to observe all things that I have commanded you; and lo, I am with you always, even to the end of the age." (Mathew 28:18-20)

TWENTY-ONE DAYS WITH GOD

A PERSONALIZED JOURNAL THROUGH THE GOSPEL OF JOHN

Twenty-one Days with God

You are beginning an adventure for the next twenty-one days. On these days you will seek to meet with God Himself through prayer and His Word. The starting place is the book of John, the Gospel of the heart of Christ.

Before you begin these exciting days, take a moment to read the following instructions. Every day you will . . .

- **Begin with a short prayer asking God to help you understand His Word.**

- **Write down a date in the space given you.** If you accidentally miss a day, do not make it up by reading two days in one—just start where you left off.

- **Read the chapter from John given for the day.** It is usually best to read the Bible in the morning, but you may find it right for you to read in the evening before you go to bed. It is helpful to read over the passage several times, if you possibly can. It will take you twenty-one days to complete the book of John.

- **Write down something special you have learned from the verses you have read.** You may discover . . . *examples* to inspire you, *promises* to encourage you, *commands* to warn you, *teachings* to instruct you and *facts* to astound you!

- **Underline in your Bible the verse you like best.**
  Take a few quiet moments to meditate on the verse.
  Fix it in your heart. Write out that verse in the
  space called "The verse I like best."

- **Record your questions.** Ask God to help you find
  the answers you need, and if you have a friend or
  mentor who will help you, ask them each week to
  talk with you about your questions and ideas.

- **Close your time alone with God by praying.** You
  may want to keep a list of the names of people and
  special needs you don't want to forget. When you
  pray, include thanks and praise to God!

- **Date** _____ Read John 1

Something important I've learned:

The verse I like best:

A question to consider:

- **Date** _____ Read John 2

Something important I've learned:

The verse I like best:

A question to consider:

- **Date** _____ Read John 3

Something important I've learned:

The verse I like best:

A question to consider:

- **Date** _____ Read John 4

Something important I've learned:

The verse I like best:

A question to consider:

_____

- **Date** _____ Read John 5

Something important I've learned:

The verse I like best:

A question to consider:

- **Date** _____ Read John 6

Something important I've learned:

The verse I like best:

A question to consider:

- **Date** _____ Read John 7

Something important I've learned:

The verse I like best:

A question to consider:

- **Date** _____ Read John 8

Something important I've learned:

The verse I like best:

A question to consider:

- **Date** _____ Read John 9

Something important I've learned:

The verse I like best:

A question to consider:

- **Date** _____ Read John 10

Something important I've learned:

The verse I like best:

A question to consider:

_____

- **Date** _____ Read John 11

Something important I've learned:

The verse I like best:

A question to consider:

- **Date** _____ Read John 12

Something important I've learned:

The verse I like best:

A question to consider:

- **Date** _____ Read John 13

Something important I've learned:

The verse I like best:

A question to consider:

- **Date** _____ Read John 14

Something important I've learned:

The verse I like best:

A question to consider:

- **Date** _____ Read John 15

Something important I've learned:

The verse I like best:

A question to consider:

- **Date** _____ Read John 16

Something important I've learned:

The verse I like best:

A question to consider:

_____

- **Date** _____ Read John 17

Something important I've learned:

The verse I like best:

A question to consider:

- **Date** _____ Read John 18

Something important I've learned:

The verse I like best:

A question to consider:

- **Date** _____ Read John 19

Something important I've learned:

The verse I like best:

A question to consider:

- **Date** _____ Read John 20

Something important I've learned:

The verse I like best:

A question to consider:

- **Date** _____ Read John 21

Something important I've learned:

The verse I like best:

A question to consider:

Here Are Some Suggestions for Completing the New Testament

- If you choose to read one chapter a day, you will finish the New Testament in less than nine months! But if you decide it is best for you to take two or three days to read some chapters, that is perfectly all right also.

- Don't let anything keep you from this important time each day. "Build your day around the Word."

- If you do miss a day, do not make it up. Just begin where you left off.

- You may decide to read the books of the New Testament in a different order than they are arranged in the Bible. Some books are more difficult than others and are of varying lengths. Just make sure you complete each book you start before going on to another book.

- Make your own notebook in order to write down what you've learned. Include "Something special I've learned," "The verse I liked best," and "A question to consider" for each section of Scripture you read. Add a section for your prayer list as well. You may wish to personalize your plan to fit you better.

- Don't be afraid to write in your Bible.

- When you have completed the New Testament, you will be ready to increase your reading to include both the New and the Old Testaments. The Lord will guide you as to what amount of reading is best for you. Read faithfully and continue to record your findings in your notebook. Perhaps one chapter in each Testament would be best (or even two if God is leading you), but do not commit yourself to more than you will be able to do. God is not in a hurry. He is interested in quality.

- Ask God to give you someone you can encourage by introducing him or her to *Pursuing God—A Seeker's Guide*. God may use you to help a friend understand how to find life in Christ.